Anne Harvey

THE GRAVEYARD WIT

The Graveyard Wit

THE HUMOUR OF THE TOMBSTONE

Compiled by Peter Haining

WITH A FOREWORD BY SPIKE MILLIGAN

"Oh, the grave!—the grave!—It buries every error—covers every defect—extinguishes every resentment."

WASHINGTON IRVING

FRANK GRAHAM

6 Queen's Terrace, Newcastle upon Tyne, 2

For
MICHAEL O'SULLIVAN & JEFF FISHER
'Comrades-in-ale'
In memory of many a good memory.

© Peter Haining 1973

First published 1973

SBN 902833 68 5

Composed in 10-pt Plantin on 12-pt body and printed in
Great Britain by Northumberland Press Limited, Gateshead

CONTENTS

INTRODUCTION

"Here lie the Dead and here the living *lie*."

ANON.

There is a story still told in Ireland about a certain Patrick O'Brien who was out strolling one day with a friend when he came across a graveyard and noticed in it a tombstone bearing the legend:

"Weep not for me, my children dear;
I am not dead, but sleeping here."

Pausing to survey the epitaph for a moment, O'Brien eventually turned to his companion and rejoined sharply: "Well, at least if I was dead I would be honest enough to admit it!"

It may come as a surprise to most people that humour is to be found in that—seemingly—most humourless of places, the graveyard. We might well expect to find high-sounding verses of praise on the graves of heroes and distinguished citizens—but humour, surely not!

However, as this little book will prove, this is far from the truth. Numerous men, women and children have been immortalised on their last resting places by ornately carved and decorated inscriptions that range from the slyly sarcastic to the uproariously funny. And this is not just a quirk of the modern age, for if we care to trace the evolvement of the graveyard epitaph we find it firmly entrenched in the earliest times.

Records show that the custom of putting inscriptions on tombstones was introduced into England by the Romans after their invasion. Understandably, therefore, we find that up to the Twelfth Century most of the epitaphs are in Latin, to be superceded surprisingly in the Thirteenth and Fourteenth Centuries by French. It is not until some years after this that the English language finally comes into widespread use.

The earliest humorous inscriptions go back almost as far as this, but they seem to have reached a peak of popularity—if such a descrip-

7

tion can be applied—in the Eighteenth Century, dropping away a little after that.

An anonymous writer of the Eighteenth Century evaluating the epitaph in a notably bloodcurdling volume entitled *The Thesaurus of Horror*; or, *The Terrors of Being Buried Alive*, said it should be short enough for everybody to read, simple enough for everybody to understand and pungent enough for everybody to remember. He felt also that it should be written in the vernacular of the locality so that it might be intelligible to fellow-countrymen with possibly a Latin copy beneath so that 'foreigners and future generations may benefit from its wisdom or wit'.

It has been my pleasure and pursuit over a good many years now to go in search of these examples of graveyard wit and the distillation of my researches is now assembled here. The epitaphs have been collected from cemeteries and graveyards throughout the British Isles, and while I would not claim the book to be definitive, it certainly does give extensive and exhaustive coverage of the humour, ribaldry and fun to be found on our tombstones.

I must hasten to add, however, that I have not personally *seen* every item quoted (a goodly number having been supplied by like-minded searchers after epitaphiania, the rest being taken from old books, newspapers and pamphlets) and I cannot therefore guarantee the validity of every verse. Some just have to be down-right suspect, but they were so amusing that I simply could not leave them out! Let me say, too, that finding the inscription is not often easy and the intrepid searcher after grave thoughts will have to frequently steel himself to plunge into dense undergrowth or explore remote, dark corners in his quest.

During my work on this book I have several times come across an identical epitaph turning up in more than one churchyard—perhaps the length of the country apart. In these cases I have quoted herein the example most easily accessible. I have also been continually astonished at the talent and imagination displayed both in the construction of the tombstone and in the wording to be found on it. It is sad that such a rich vein of native art should so often be discarded, overgrown and unvisited. If just a few more people should feel inclined to explore a few more graveyards and thereby experience one more facet of the great English trait for eccentricity, I shall feel this book had been worthwhile. (The Editor and Publisher would also welcome any further epitaphs which readers may be aware of, or uncover, particularly those from the Northern Counties of North-umberland, Durham, Cumberland, Westmorland, Lancashire and Yorkshire, as a companion volume *The Northern Graveyard Wit* is now in preparation.)

Here, then, are the dead-but-not-forgotten who have left a legacy of laughter for us all to enjoy ... and perhaps profit by.

PETER A. HAINING
Birch Green,
Essex.

My Epitaph by Spike Milligan

FOREWORD

by Spike Milligan

Since time began, man has held death in various states of emotional and intellectual dilemma and awe. What was it, an end? or a beginning?

The most positive thing he's done, in fact, is to disdain it; i.e. great acts of heroism in the face of danger. Even to this day, the greatest and most revered awards are ones for heroism—in America, the Congressional Medal of Honour, and our own, older, Victoria Cross.

But, in many philosophies (and my own) the answer is laughter, yet this has only been a comparatively recent innovation in man's approach to death. Round about AD 1500 mildly humorous remarks started to appear in English on tombstones—

> Here lyes Margaret Young
> Who had shee lived
> Would surely been hung
> By the length of her tongue.

Now this was a daring innovation when you consider the awe of, say, *Australopithecus*, who reverently bound the deceased in the sitting position, smeared the corpse with red clay, and hoped that the colour and position of the body might deceive the Doppel-ganger into believing the corpse to be still alive. Or, in contrast, the incredible finery of the dead Pharaohs. The thought of a comic comment on the pyramids would have been greeted with horror, even death.

But, as I say, since 1500(ish) there has been a genuine progress in cutting back the 'Reapers' grisly image by a change of emphasis, until, in 1800, you get genuine comic gems like this:

> Here lies the body
> Of Mabel Charlotte
> Born a virgin
> Died a harlot.

11

She was a virgin
Till her 21st year
A remarkable thing
In Oxfordshire.

It shows us a psychological courage as against the obvious physical one; for the hero who beat death, the danger was over—but the village joker who ammended the following epitaph:

Pray you all
For the Vicar's daughter
Millicent Ann
Who died as pure
As the day she began

—then added:

Not afore, in this village,
She had every man

must have looked over his shoulder of a dark night for many a year!

I myself have never desecrated a tombstone, not even in fun, but I have had cause to concoct an epitaph. During the Second World War in North Africa I befriended a wild dog which we called Havelock Ellis. No one was sadder than I when he was shot in the head one dark night when he attacked a sentry, so I put pen to paper and wrote:

Here lies the body
Of Havelock the dog
Shot thru the head
And dropped like a log.
If he'd have been smart
And not bit Gunner Fred
This little dog
Would not be dead.

I was heartbroken at his death—and yet it seemed better he had a funny epitaph when he died.

Man will forever be battling against death—sometimes with horrific results. I have seen old people who were no more than slow-pulsing vegetables—*they* wanted to go. *If* they had been told they were going to be put to sleep they would have been *happy*.

There is a time to live, a time to die, a time to laugh, and at no time are the three of them very far apart. I myself have my epitaph. It will read:

"I demand a second opinion"

So read this book then—it has obviously been put together with love and gales of laughter, and buy a few for your friends, the older the better. Why not lay down in the garden with this book and a shovel, and make up your own epitaph? Better still, make up one about some-one you hate, like the Inland Revenue:

> The man who ruined me for life
> Was this damn Tax Inspector
> But he tripped and fell upon a knife
> And now he's just a spectre.

And remember, you'll never get to heaven alive!

ILLUSTRATIONS

I

Some Curious Characters

Here lies the bones of WILLIAM JONES,
  Who, when alive, collected bones;
But Death, that bony, grizzly spectre,
  That most amazing bone collector,
Has boned poor JONES so snug and tidy,
  That here he lies in *bona fide*.

        St. Lawrence's Church
        Isle of Wight.

★

Here lies the body of barren PEG,
  Who had no issue but one in her leg;
But while she was living she was so cunning,
That when one stood still the other was running.

        Stanmore Churchyard,
        Middlesex.

★

Here lies interr'd a man o' micht,
  His name was MALCOLM DOWNIE;
He lost his life, ae market nicht,
  By fa'in' off his pownie.

        Cullen Graveyard,
        Banffshire.

★

Here lies ANN MANN
She lived an old maid
And died an old Mann.

> Barton Moss Cemetery,
> nr. Manchester,
> Lancashire.

★

Here lies romantic PHOEBE,
  Half Ganymede, half Hebe;
A Maid of mutable condition,
  A jockey, cowherd and musician.

> From the tombstone of
> Phoebe Brown at Matlock,
> Derbyshire.

★

Whoever treadeth on this stone
I prey you tread most neatly
For underneath this same do lie
Your honest friend—WILL WHEATLY

> Stepney Cemetery,
> London.

★

17

Underneath this stone lies MEREDITH MORGAN,
Who blew the bellows of our church organ.
Tobacco he hated, to smoke most unwilling,
Yet never so pleased as when pipes he was filling.
No reflection on him for rude speech could be cast,
Though he gave our old organ many a blast!
No puffer was he, though a capital blower;
He could blow double G, and now lies a note lower.

Llanfylantwthyl Parish Church,
Wales.

★

*Here lies the body of LADY O'LOONEY, great
neice of Burke. She was bland, passionate
and deeply religious; also she painted in water
colours. She was first cousin of Lady Jones
and of such is the Kingdom of Heaven.*

Bridgewater Cemetery,
Somerset.

★

Here lyes STEPHEN RUMBOLD
He lived to ye age of 100 & 1
Sanguine & Strong:
An hundred to one
You don't live so long

Brightwell Baldwin Church,
Oxfordshire.

★

18

Here lies HONEST NED,
Because he is dead.
Had it been his father,
We had much rather;
Had it been his mother,
We had rather than the other;
Had it been his sister,
We ne'er should have missed her:
But since it is only Ned,
There's no more to be said.

Kirkby Stephen Parish Church,
Westmorland.

*

Near this place is interred
THEODORE, King of Corsica,
Who died in this Parish
December XI., MDCCLVI.,
Immediately after leaving
The *King's Bench Prison,*
By the benefit of the *Act of Insolvency*;
In consequence of which
He *registered his Kingdom of Corsica*
For the use of his Creditors!

The grave—great teacher—to a level brings
Heroes and beggars, galley-slaves and kings!
But THEODORE this moral learned, ere dead;
Fate pour'd its lessons on his living head,
Bestow'd a kingdom, and denied him bread.

St. Anne's Church,
Soho, London.

*

19

Here lies the good old knight SIR HARRY,
Who loved well, but would not marry.

From the grave of a notorious
womaniser at Ditchley Parish
Church, Oxfordshire.

★

FIVE
TIMES HE WIVED
BUT STILL SURVIVED
TO SEEK A SIXTH HE AT
THE AGE OF 93 WALKED TO
LONDON TOWN BUT THE JOURNEY GOT HIM DOWN.

The tombstone of Nicholas Toke
in Kensington Cemetery, London.

★

Here lies ROGER RUTTER alias RUDDER
who was buried August 30 1771, aged 84 years,
having never eaten FLESH, FISH or FOWL
during the course of his long life.

Uley Churchyard,
Gloucestershire.

★

Here lies the Earl of Suffolk's fool,
  Men called him DICKY PEARCE;
    His folly serv'd to make men laugh,
      When wit and mirth were scarce.
        Poor Dick, alas! is dead and gone,
          What signifies to cry?
            Dickys' enough are still behind
            To laugh at by and by.

                    Beckley Church,
                    Suffolk.

                    ★

Sacred to the memory of a character
            JOHN CAMERON
            "Johnnie Laddie"
a native of Campbeltown, Scotland, who
died there August 26, 1858, aged 65 years.
Erected to his memory by public subscription.

        Sixty winters on the street,
        No shoes nor stockings on his feet;
        Amusement both to small and great,
          Was poor "Johnnie Laddie".

                    Campbeltown Parish Church,
                    Scotland.

                    ★

            So died JOHN SO,
            So so did he so?
            So did he live
            And So did he die;
            So so did he so?
            And So let him lie.

                    From the grave of a recluse
                    in St. John's Church, Glasgow.

                    ★

                    21

On the following tombstone is affixed an iron dish:

Here lies my corpse, who was the man
That loved a sop in the dripping pan;
But now believe me, I am dead,
See how the pan stands at my head,
Still for the sops till the last I cried,
But could not eat, and so I died.
My neighbours, they perhaps will laugh
When they do read my epitaph.

> Woodditton nr. Newmarket,
> Suffolk.

★

ONCE I WAS ALIVE
AND HAD FLESH, DID THRIVE
BUT NOW I AM A SKELLITANT AT 70.

> From the gravestone of an old
> eccentric who called himself
> "The King of Jerusalem" and is
> buried at Sunningdale Church,
> Berkshire.

★

Stranger! Behold interred together
The souls of learning and of leather.
Poor JOE is gone, but left his awl
You'll find his relics in a stall.

> From the grave of Joseph
> Blackett, a shoe-maker and
> would-be poet, at Seaham
> Parish Church, Durham.

★

Beneath the gravel and these stones,
Lies poor JACK TIFFEY'S skin and bones,
His flesh I oft have heard him say,
He hoped in time would make good hay;
Quoth I, "How can that come to pass?"
And he replied, "All flesh is grass!"

Pickering Cemetery,
Yorkshire.

★

23

II

'Till Death Us Do Part'

Wives

This spot's the sweetest
I've seen in my life
For it raises my flowers
And covers my wife.

> Llanelly Cemetery,
> Wales.

★

Underneath this sod lies ARABELLA YOUNG,
Who on the 5th of May began to hold her tongue.

> Chester Parish Church,
> Cheshire.

★

My wife is dead and here she lies,
Nobody laughs and nobody cries;
Where she is gone to or how she fares,
Nobody knows and nobody cares.

> Painswick Parish Church,
> nr. Stroud, Gloucestershire.

★

CHARITY, wife of Gideon BLIGH,
Underneath this stone doth lie,
Naught was she ever known to do
That her husband told her to.

> St. Michael Penkevil Church,
> Devonshire.

★

This stone was raised to SARAH FORD
Not Sarah's virtues to record
For they're well known by all the town
No, Lord, it was raised to keep her down.

> Kilmurry Cemetery,
> Scotland.

★

TO THE MEMORY OF SUSAN MUM:—
SILENCE IS WISDOM.

> Nelson Parish Church,
> nr. Burnley, Lancashire.

★

27

Who far below this tomb dost rest,
Has joined the army of the blest,
The Lord has ta'en her to the sky:
The saints rejoice, and so do I.

Cherening-le-Clay Churchyard,
Dorsetshire.

*

Here snug in grave my wife doth lie,
Now she's at rest and so am I.

Old Grey Friars Cemetery,
Edinburgh.

*

Here lies my wife,
  In earthy mould,
Who, when she lived,
  Did naught but scold.
Good friends go softly
  In your walking
Lest she should wake
  And rise up talking.

Ponteland,
Northumberland.

*

Here lie the bodies

Of THOMAS BOND, and MARY his Wife.

She was temperate, chaste, and charitable;

But, she was proud, peevish, and passionate.

She was an affectionate wife, and a tender mother;

But, her husband and child, whom she loved,

seldom saw her countenance without a disgusting frown,

whilst she received visitors, whom she despised, with

an endearing smile.

Her behaviour was discreet towards strangers;

But imprudent in her family.

Abroad, her conduct was influenced by good breeding;

But, at home, by ill temper.

She was a professed enemy to flattery,

and was seldom known to praise or commend;

But, the talents in which she principally excelled

were differences of opinion, and discovering

flaws and imperfections.

She was an admirable economist, and, without prodigality,

dispensed plenty to every person in her family;

But, would sacrifice their eyes to a farthing candle.

She sometimes made her husband happy with her good

qualities;

But, much more frequently miserable with her many

failings;

Insomuch, that in thirty years' cohabitation

he often lamented

that, maugre all her virtues,

he had not, in the whole, enjoyed two

years of matrimonial comfort.

At length, finding she had lost the affection of her

husband, as well as the regard of her neighbours,

family disputes having been divulged by servants,

she died of vexation, *July* 20, 1768, aged 48 years.

Her worn-out husband survived her four months and two

days,

and departed this life *Nov.* 28th 1768,

in the 54th year of his age.

WILLIAM BOND, Brother to the deceased,

erected this stone
as a *weekly monitor* to the surviving
wives of this parish,
that they may avoid the infamy
of having their *memories* handed down to posterity
with a patch-work character.

Horsleydown Church,
Cumberland.

＊

I am safe in saying
She's gone up higher,
Nary a devil would want Maria.

Ubley Church,
Somerset.

＊

Beneath this silent stone is laid
A noisy, antiquated maid,
Who from her cradle talk'd till death,
And ne'er before was out of breath.

Falkirk Cemetery,
Scotland.

＊

Here lies my wife EDIE,
Who in her time made me giddy;
Here she lies without bed or blanket,
As dead as a door-nail, the Lord be thanked.

> Tiddington Church,
> Oxford.

★

Here lies the body of MARY FORD
We hope her soul is with the Lord.
But if for Hell she's changed this life
Better live there than as J. Ford's wife.

> Sowerby Churchyard,
> Yorkshire.

★

God be praised;
Here is Mr. DUDLEY senior,
And JANE his wife also,
Who, while living, was his superior,
But see what death can do.

> Broom Parish Churchyard,
> Worcestershire.

★

31

Here lies the man RICHARD,
    And MARY his wife;
Their surname was PRITCHARD,
    They lived without strife.
And the reason was plain:
    They abounded in riches,
They had no care or pain,
And the wife wore the breeches.

> Chelmsford Cathedral,
> Essex.

★

Here lies the body of SARAH SEXTON
She was a wife that never vexed one.
    I can't say as much
    For the first one
Underneath the next stone.

> Memorial to a second wife
> at Falkirk, Scotland.

★

Two great physicians first
My loving husband tried,
To cure my pain—
In vain
At last he got a third
And then I died.

> From the grave of Molly Dickie
> in Cheltenham Graveyard, Gloucs.

★

Perhaps the most famous of all sextons, 'Old Scarlett' of Peterborough Cathedral, who died in July 1591 aged 98. An engraving from his tombstone.

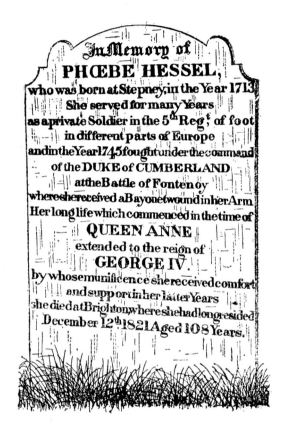

In Memory of
PHŒBE HESSEL,
who was born at Stepney, in the Year 1713.
She served for many Years
as a private Soldier in the 5th Reg.t of foot
in different parts of Europe
and in the Year 1745 fought under the command
of the DUKE of CUMBERLAND
at the Battle of Fontenoy
where she received a Bayonet wound in her Arm
Her long life which commenced in the time of
QUEEN ANNE
extended to the reign of
GEORGE IV.
by whose munificence she received comfort
and support in her latter Years
she died at Brighton where she had long resided
December 12th 1821 Aged 108 Years.

The tombstone of Phoebe Hessel, a remarkable
'woman at arms' who lived to be 108 and is buried
in Brighton Churchyard, Sussex.

Censure not rashly, though nature's apt to halt,
No woman's born that dies without a fault.

St. Mary's Church,
Islington, London.

Husbands

STRANGER CALL THIS NOT
   A PLACE OF GLOOM.
TO ME IT IS A PLEASANT SPOT
   MY HUSBAND'S TOMB.

Cockermouth,
Cumberland.

★

Here let a bard unenvied rest,
Who no dull critic dares molest;
Escaped from the familiar ills
Of thread-bare coat and unpaid bills;
From rough bum-bailiff's upstart duns,
From sneering pride's detested sons,
From all those pest'ring ills of life,
From worse than all, a scolding wife.

Houghton-on-the-Hill
Churchyard, Leicestershire.

★

Three of her husbands slumber here.
This turf has drunk a widow's tear:

> Barton Under Needwood Church,
> Staffordshire.

★

She lived with her husband 50 years
And died in the confident hope of a better life.

> Easingwold Church,
> Yorkshire.

★

HERE LIES JOHN HILL,
  A MAN OF SKILL,
WHOSE AGE WAS FIVE TIMES TEN:
  HE NEVER DID GOOD,
  AND NEVER WOULD,
IF HE LIVED AS LONG AGAIN.

> Bishop Auckland,
> Durham.

★

Here lies JEMMY LITTLE, a carpenter industrious
A very good-natured man, but somewhat blusterous.
When that his little wife his authority withstood
He took a little stick and banged her as he would.
His wife now left alone, her loss does so deplore,
She wishes Jemmy back to bang her a little more;
For now he's dead and gone this fault appears so small,
A little thing would make her think it was no fault
                                                        at all.

                              Portsmouth Cemetery,
                              Hampshire.

                    ★

         Great was my grief, I could not rest
         God called me hence—thought it best;
            Unhappy marriage was my fate,
         I did repent when it was too late.

                              St. Alban's Cemetery,
                              Hertfordshire.

                    ★

Oh cruel Death! why wert thou so unkind,
To take the one, and leave the other behind?
Thou should'st have taken both or neither,
Which would have been more agreeable to the survivor.

                              Birmingham,
                              Warwickshire.

                    ★

                    37

Here lays JOHN, with MARY his bride,
They lived and they laugh'd while they were able,
And at last were obliged to knock under the table.

Harrogate Cemetery,
Yorkshire.

★

In Memory of
JOHN DALE
Know, all posterity, that in the year
of grace 1757, the rambling remains of
the above said John Dale were laid
UPON HIS TWO WIVES
This thing in life might cause some jealousy:
Here all three lay together lovingly;
But from embraces here no pleasure flows,
Alike are here all human joys and woes.
Here old John's rambling Sarah no more fears.
And Elizabeth's chiding he no longer hears;
A period's come to all their toilsome lives;
The good man's quiet. Still are both his wives.

Bakewell Parish Church,
Derbyshire.

★

Here lies the body of JAMES ROBINSON
and RUTH his wife
"THEIR WARFARE IS ACCOMPLISHED."

St. Saviour's Church,
London, N.9.

III

Sportsmen

I bowl'd, I struck, I stopp'd,
   Sure life's a game of cricket,
I blocked with care, with caution popp'd,
   Yet death has hit my wicket.

               Salisbury Cemetery,
               Wiltshire.

★

Death took him in the *upper View*
   And gave him such a *Brace,*
The grapple turn'd him black and blue,
   And made him shift his place.
Parts of Access he next assailed,
   With such a *Knock-Down Blow*
As never yet to mortal fail'd
   A total overthrow.

               From the long decayed grave
               of a London wrestling champion.

★

Here lies the pugilist
JAMES EARL
who on the 11th of April 1788
gave in

               Battersea Cemetery,
               London.

★

Here lies the body of WILLIAM BECK
He was thrown at a hunt and broke his neck.

Ipswich Cemetery,
Suffolk.

★

This is to the memory of OLD AMOS
Who was when alive for hunting famous;
But now his chases are all o'er
And here he's earth'd of years four score.
Upon this tomb he's often sat
And tried to read his epitaph;
And thou who dost so at this moment
Shall ere long like him be dormant.

From the tombstone of the
celebrated Yorkshire huntsman
Amos Street, in Birstal
churchyard.

★

Here lies JOHN MILLS, who over the hills
Pursued the hounds with hallo;
The leap though high, from earth to sky
The huntsman we must follow.

Caldbeck Parish Church,
Cumberland.

★

My gun discharged, my ball is gone,
My powder's spent, my work is done,
Those panting deer I have left behind
May now have time to gain their wind.
Since I, who off have chased them o'er,
The verdant plains, am now no more.

> East Hucknell Churchyard,
> Derbyshire.

★

Here lies an Old Toss'd Tennis Ball,
  Was Racketted from Spring to Fall
With so much heat and so much blast
  Time's arm (for shame) grew tyr'd at last.

> From the grave of tennis
> enthusiast Gervase Scrope
> in Coventry Cemetery,
> Warwickshire.

★

Here lies a marksman, who with art and skill,
  When young and strong, fat bucks and does did kill.
Now conquered by grim Death (go, reader, tell it!)
He's now took leave of powder, gun and pellet.
  A fatal dart, which in the dark did fly,
    Has laid him down, among the dead to lie.

> Ravenglass Parish Church,
> Westmorland.

★

Here lies TOMMY MONTAGUE
Whose love for angling daily grew;
He died regretted, while late out,
    To make a capture of a trout.

                Sutton Mallet Cemetery,
                Somerset.

                    ★

His net old fisher GEORGE long drew,
    Shoals upon shoals he caught,
Till Death came hauling for his due
    And made poor George his draught.

                Hythe Parish Church,
                Kent.

                    ★

HOOK'D IT.

                From an angler's grave, now
                disappeared, in the Parish
                Church of St. Mary's, Swansea.

IV

Professional People

Actresses

HERE, READER, YOU MAY PLAINLY SEE,
THAT WIT NOR HUMOUR HERE COULD BE
A PROOF AGAINST MORTALITY.

> From the grave of Henrietta
> Maria Bray at Mancroft Parish
> Church, Norwich.

★

This we must own in justice to her shade,
'Twas the first bad exit OLDFIELD ever made.

> From the tombstone of dramatic
> actress, Mrs. Oldfield, in
> Brixton, London.

★

Oh, sad to tell
On Mrs. MONKS
The curtain last has fell.

> Stratford Cemetery,
> London.

★

Here early to bed lies kind WILLIAM MAGINN
He turn'd author ere yet there was beard on his chin,
But to save from starvation stirr'd never a pin,
He got leave to die here, out of Babylon's din,
Barring drink and the girls, I ne'er heard of a sin,
　Many worse, better few, than bright, broken MAGINN.

　　　　　Walton-on-Thames Parish Church,
　　　　　Surrey.

★

Here lies FRANCIS GROSE
On Thursday, May 12 1791
Death put an end to his
Views and *Prospects*!

　　　　　From the tomb of the author of
　　　　　several topographical works in
　　　　　Canterbury Cemetery, Kent.

★

Here lies poor NED PARDON, from misery free,
　Who long was a bookseller's hack;
He led such a damnable life in this world,
　I don't think he'll ever come back.

　　　　　St. Bride's Church,
　　　　　London.

★

47

Baker

RICHARD FULLER lies buried here;
   Do not withold the crystal tear;
For when he lived he daily fed
   Woman, and man and child, with bread.
But now, alas; he's turn'd to dust,
   As thou, and I, and all soon must;
And lies beneath this turn so green,
   Where worms do daily feed on him,

> Pontefract Graveyard,
> Yorkshire.

★

Bellows-makers

Here lyeth JOHN CRUKER, a maker of bellowes,
His craftes-master and right good fellowe;
Yet when he came to the hour of his death,
He that made bellowes, could not make breath.

> Accrington Cemetery,
> Lancashire.

★

Blown Up Afar
JOHN WINDING, Bellows-maker.

> Moffat Churchyard,
> Dumfriesshire.

★

Here lies ROBERT WALLAS,
The King of Good Fellows,
Clerk of All-Hallows,
And maker of bellows.

All Saints' Church,
Newcastle-on-Tyne,
Northumberland.

*

Blacksmith

Here cool the ashes of MULCIBER GRIM
Late of this Parish, Blacksmith;
He was born in Seacole Lane, and bred at Hammersmith.
From his youth upwards he was much addicted
to vices, and was often guilty of forgery.
Having some talents for irony,
He therefore produced many heats in his neighbourhood,
which he usually increased by blowing up the coals.
This rendered him so unpopular that when he found
it necessary to adopt cooling measures,
His conduct was generally accompanied with a hiss.
Though he sometimes proved a warm friend, yet, where
his interest was concerned, he made it a constant
rule to strike while the iron was hot, regardless of
the injury he might do thereby;
And when he had
any matter of moment upon the anvil he seldom failed
to turn it to his own advantage.
Among the numberless instances that might be given of
the cruelty of his disposition, it need only be
mentioned
That he was the means of hanging many of the innocent
family of the Bells,
Under the idle pretence of keeping them from jangling;

49

And put great numbers of the hearts of Steel into
the hottest flames,
merely (as he declared) to soften the obduracy of
their tempers.
At length, after passing a long life in the commission
of these black actions, his fire being exhausted,
and his bellows worn out,
He filed off to that place where only the fervid
ordeal of
his own forge can be exceeded:
Declaring with his last puff, that man is born to
trouble as the sparks fly upwards.

Sherborne Church,
Dorsetshire.

★

Butcher

Here lies a true and honest man,
You scarce would find such a one in ten;
For killing pigs was his delight,
Which art he practised day and night.

Cheltenham Parish Church,
Gloucestershire.

★

The grave of the 'Sage of Chelsea' a vain
Scottish eccentric who died from the
effects of wearing her stays too tightly
laced! In the churchyard at Springkell
near Ecclefechan, Dumfrieshire.

Kicked to death by a horse—from the
grave in Melton Mowbray Parish Church,
Oxford.

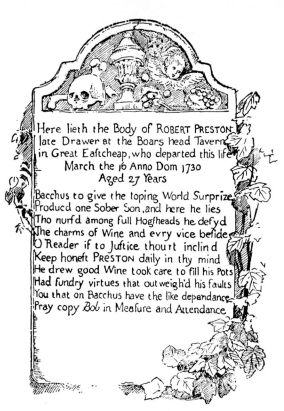

Here lieth the Body of ROBERT PRESTON
late Drawer at the Boars head Tavern
in Great Eaftcheap, who departed this life
March the 16 Anno Dom 1730
Aged 27 Years

Bacchus to give the toping World Surprize
Produc'd one Sober Son, and here he lies
Tho nurf'd among full Hogfheads he defy'd
The charms of Wine and evry vice befide
O Reader if to Juftice thou'rt inclin'd
Keep honeft PRESTON daily in thy mind
He drew good Wine took care to fill his Pots
Had fundry virtues that outweigh'd his faults
You that on Bacchus have the like dependance
Pray copy Bob in Meafure and Attendance

A non-drinker among drinkers at St. Michael's Church, Eastcheap, London.

MARTHA BLEWIT,
of the Swan Inn at Bathorn-End
in this Parish,
buried May 7th 1681:
was the Wife of nine Hufbands fuccefsively.
but the ninth outlived her.
The Text to her Funeral Sermon was
"Laft of all the Woman died alfo."
ROBERT HOGAN
of this Parish
was the Hufband of Seven Wives fuccefsively,
he married Ann Livermore his seventh Wife
January 1. 1739.

A much-married pair to be found at Birdbrook Church, Haverhill, Essex.

Cardmaker

His card is cut: long days he shuffled through
the game of life: he dealt as others do.
Though he by honours tells not its amount,
When the last trump is played, his tricks will count.

Manchester,
Lancashire.

★

Carpenter

Who many a sturdy oak has laid along,
Fell'd by Death's surer hatchet her lies JOHN SPONG
Post oft he made, yet ne'er a place could get
    And lived by railing, tho' he was no wit.
Old saws he had, although no antiquarian;
And stiles corrected, yet was no grammarian.
    Long lived he Ockham's favourite architect,
        And lasting as his fame a tomb t'erect,
        In vain we seek an artist such as he,
Whose pales and piles were for eternity.

Ockham Churchyard,
Surrey.

★

HURRAH! MY BOYS, AT THE PARSON'S FALL,
FOR IF HE'D LIVED, HE'D A-BURIED US ALL.

> Taibach Churchyard,
> South Wales.

★

Beneath this spot lies buried
One CHEST within another,
The outer chest was a good one:
Who says so of the other?

> From the tomb of a disgraced
> Chepstow, London, clergyman,
> Rev. John Chest.

★

Here lies a Cardinal, who wrought
  Both good and evil in his time;
The good he did was good for nought;
  Not so the evil! That was prime.

> Preston Cemetery,
> Lancashire.

★

You see OLD SCARLETT'S picture stand on hie;
But at your feet here doth his body lye.
His gravestone doth his age and death-time shew,
His office by his token(s) you may know.
Second to none for strength and sturdy lymm,
A scare-babe mighty voice, with visage grim;
He had inter'd two queenes within this place,
And this townes householders in his life's space
Twice over; but at length his own time came
What he for others did, for him the same
was done; no doubt his soule doth live for aye,
In heaven, though his body clad in clay.

Peterborough Cathedral.

★

Here lies the body of poor FRANK RAW
    Parish clerk and gravestone cutter
    And this is writ to let you know
What Frank for others used to do
    Is now for Frank done by another.

Selby Churchyard,
Yorkshire.

★

Here lies JAMES WILLIAMSON
Who died September 6th 1812.
For piety he did excel and
        of all the elders,
Of his sect, he bore the bell,
Of every web he wove
        he stole an ell.

Dunfermline Cemetery,
Scotland.

★

55

The graves around for many a year
Were dug by him who slumbers here,
Till worn with age, he dropped his spade
And in the dust his bones were laid.

Hartwith Chapel, Nidderdale,
Yorkshire.

★

In the memory of HEZEKIAH BRIGGS
Who died in the 80th year of his age
He was Sexton at this church 43 years
And interred upwards of 7,000 corpses.

Bingley Parish Church,
Yorkshire.

★

He that carried many a body brave,
Was carried by a fever to the grave;
He carried, and was carried; that's even:
Lord! make him Porter to the gates of Heaven!

Hexham Parish Church,
Northumberland.

★

Here lies JOHN WHEEDLE, Parish Beedle,
  Who was so very knowing;
His wisdom's gone and so is he
  Because he's left off growing.

> St. Nicholas Church, Yarmouth,
> Isle of Wight.

*

HERE LIES ONE
BLOWN OUT OF BREATH
WHO LIVED A MERRY LIFE
AND DIED A *MERIDETH*

> The gravestone of Mr. Merideth,
> organist at St. James's Church,
> Oxford.

*

Comedian

FOOTE from his earthly stage, alas! is hurled:
Death took him off who took off all the world.

> From the grave of the London
> comedian, Mr. Foote.

*

Underneath this crust,
Lies the mouldering dust of
   ELEANOR BATCHELOR SHOVEN,
   Well versed in the Arts
Of pies, custards and tarts,
And the lucrative trade of the oven.
When she lived long enough
   She made her last puff,
A puff by her husband much praised,
   And now she doth lie
   And make a dirt pie,
In hopes that her crust may be raised.

               Whitby Parish Church,
               Yorkshire.

★

PEAS TO HIS HASHES;
MEANING OF COURSE,
PEACE TO HIS ASHES.

               Longridge Cemetery,
               Nr. Preston,
               Lancashire.

★

Alas, alas! WILL SCRIVENOR'S dead, who by his art
Could make Death's Skeleton edible in each part.
More squeamish stomachs, and ye curious Palates,
You've lost your dainty dishes and your Salades:
Mourn for yourselves, but not for him in the least,
He's gone to taste of a more Heavenly Feast.

> Kings Lynn Cemetery,
> Norfolk.

★

Coroner

He lived
And died
By suicide.

> From the grave of a Coroner
> who hanged himself at West
> Grinstead, London.

★

Criminal

Here lies the body of Thomas Kemp,
Who lived by wool and died by hemp;
There's nothing would suffice this glutton,
But with the fleece to steal the mutton;
Had he but worked and lived uprighter,
He'd ne'er been hung for a sheep-biter.

> Bellingham Parish Churchyard,
> Northumberland.

★

Dentist

STRANGER, TREAD THIS GROUND WITH GRAVITY
DENTIST BROWN IS FILLING HIS LAST CAVITY.

> St. George's Church,
> Edinburgh.

★

Dustman

> Beneath yon humble clod at rest,
> Lies ANDREW, who, if not the best,
>   Was not the very worst man;
> A little rakish, apt to roam,
> But not so now, he's quite at home,
>   For Andrew was a Dustman.

> Edinburgh,
> Scotland.

★

Dyer

> Here lies a man who first did dye,
>   When he was twenty-four,
> And yet he lived to reach the age
>   Of hoary hairs, fourscore,
> But now he's gone and certain 'tis
> He'll not dye any more.

> St. Nicholas Church,
> Yarmouth.

★

Grocer

Here lie the remains of JOHN HALL, grocer.
The world is not worth a fig and I have good raisins
For saying so.

> Dunmore Churchyard,
> Ireland.

★

Highwayman

My friends, here I am—Death at last has prevail'd
   And for once all my projects are baffled,
'Tis a blessing to know, tho', when once a man's nailed
   He has no further dread of the scaffold.
My life was cut short by a shot thro' the head,
   On his Majesty's highway at Dalston—
So as now 'Number One's' numbered one of the dead,
   All's one if he's *Alston* or *All-stone*.

> Tombstone of Ned Alston,
> the Essex Highwayman, at
> Nayland Churchyard, Suffolk.

★

Lawyers

God works a wonder now and then,
Here, though a lawyer, was an honest man.

> Rineton Churchyard,
> Norfolk.

★

Here, reader, turn your weeping eyes,
  My fate a useful moral teaches,
The hole in which my body lies
  Would not contain one half my speeches.

> Grasmere Church,
> Westmorland.

★

This is a mere law quibble, not a wonder:
Here lies a lawyer and his client under.

> Blackpool,
> Lancashire.

★

Milkman

Milk and water sold I ever
Weight and measure, gave I never,
So to the Devil I must go,
  Woe, woe, woe, woe.

> Earls Barton Cemetery,
> Northamptonshire.

★

Musicians

Stephen and Time are now both even,
Stephen beats Time, but now Time's beaten Stephen.

> Grave of a music teacher at
> St. Ives, Cornwall.

★

When Orpheus played he moved Old Nick:
But thou only moved thy fiddle-stick.

> York Cemetery,
> Yorkshire.

★

Poets

Here lies the preacher, judge
  And poet, PETER:
Who broke the laws of
  God and Man
  And meter.

> From the grave in Bristol
> Cemetery of Peter Robinson
> J.P., Deacon and Poet.

★

Pity, not envy, be the lot
Of him who lieth here! I wot
A thousand deaths he long endured,
Until by death his ills were cured.
Stranger, pass on, and make no riot—
Take care he slumbers on in quiet,
Nor break the only sleep (t'is true!)
Unhappy SCARRON ever knew.

Tombstone of the comic
poet Scarron at Liverpool,
Lancashire.

★

Here lies JOHN and likewise MARY
 Cheek by jowl and never weary;
 No wonder they so well agree,
John wants no punch, nor Moll no tea.

From the grave of John Collier,
alias Tim Bobbin, the
Lancashire poet, in Rochdale
Cemetery.

★

Printers

Here lie the remains of L. GEDGE, Printer,
Like a worn-out character, he has returned to the Founder
Hoping that he will be re-cast in a better and
more perfect mould.

Morpeth Parish Church,
Northumberland.

★

In memori ov

MERI PITMAN

Weif ov Mr. Eizak Pitman
Fonetik Printer, ov this Siti.
Died 19 August 1857, edjed 64.
"Preper tu mit thei God."
—Ĕmos 4-12.

Epitaph in phonetic English
in Lansdown Cemetery, Bath,
Somerset.

★

Potter

Beneath this stone lies CATHERINE GRAY,
Changed to a lifeless lump of clay;
By earth and clay she got her pelf,
And now she's turned to earth herself.

Ye weeping friends, let me advise,
Abate your tears and dry your eyes;
  For what avails a flood of tears?
  Who knows but in a course of years,
  In some tall pitcher or brown pan,
    She in her shop may be again.

> Chester Cathedral,
> Cheshire.

★

Quack Doctors

I was a Quack, and there are men who say
That in my time I physicked men away,
And that at length I by myself was slain,
By my own doings te'en to relieve my pain.
The truth is, being troubled with a cough,
I, like a fool, consulted Dr. Gough,
Who physicked to death at his own will,
Because he's licensed by the State to kill.
Had I but wisely taken my own physic
I never should have died of cold and 'tisick.
So be warned, and when you catch a cold
Go to my son, by whom my medicine's sold.

> Carlisle Cemetery,
> Cumberland.

★

Here lies my adviser, Dr. Sim,
And those he healed—near him.

> Grimsby Parish Church,
> Yorkshire.

★

Railway Engineer

My engine now is cold and still,
No water does my boiler fill;
My coke affords its flame no more
My days of usefulness are o'er;
My wheels deny their noted speed,
No more my guiding hand they need:
My whistle, too, has lost its tone,
Its shrill and thrilling sounds are gone;
My valves are now thrown open wide;
My flanges all refuse to guide,
My clacks also, though once so strong,
Refuse to aid the busy throng:
No more I feel each urging breath:
My steam is now condensed in death.
Life's railway o'er each stations passed,
In death I'm stopped, and rest at last.

> Bromsgrove Churchyard,
> Worcestershire.

★

Sailor

Here lies, retired from busy scenes,
   A first lieutenant of Marines,
Who lately lived in gay content
   On board the brave ship "Diligent".
Now stripped of all his warlike show,
   And laid in box of elm below,
Confined in earth in narrow borders,
   He rises not till further orders.

                Barwick-in-Elmet Church,
                Yorkshire.

★

Servant

In memory of JOHN KING
He was 61 years servant
to Mr. Francis Valentine,
Mr. Joseph Valentine
and Mr. Paul Valentine.
From father to son
Without ever
Quitting their Service
Neglecting his duty
Or being Disguised in Liquor.

                Beckenham Church,
                Kent.

★

Shoemaker

Our bodies are like shoes, which off we cast;
Physic their cobblers; and death their last.

> Cirencester Churchyard,
> Gloucestershire.

★

Smuggler

> *Here I lies*
> *Kill'd by the XIS*

> Woodbridge Cemetery,
> Suffolk.

★

Surgeon

Here lies in repose, after great deeds of blood,
  An hospital surgeon thorough,
Who bled for his own and his country's good,
  And St. Thomas's Hospital, Borough.

> London.

★

Town Clerk

Here lies interred
Beneath these stones
The beard, the flesh
And eke the bones
Of Wrexham's Clerk
Old DANIEL JONES.

Wrexham Cemetery, Denbighshire,
Wales.

★

Watchmaker

Here lies, in horizontal position
the outside case of
GEORGE ROUTLEIGH, watchmaker;
Whose abilities in that line were an honour
to his profession.
Integrity was the Mainspring, and prudence
the Regulator,
of all the actions of his life.
Humane, generous, and liberal,
his Hand never stopped
till he had relieved distress.
So nicely regulated were all his motions
that he never went wrong,
except when set a-going
by people
who did not know his Key:
even then he was easily
set right again.
He had the art of disposing his time so well
that his hours glided away
in one continual round

of pleasure and delight,
till an unlucky minute put a period to
his existence.
He departed this life
Nov. 14 1802
aged 57:
wound up,
in hopes of being taken in hand
by his Maker;
and of being thoroughly cleaned repaired
and set a-going
in the world to come.

Lydford Church,
Dartmoor.

★

Weavers

Here lies the body of DANIEL SAUL
Spitalfields weaver—and that's all.

St. Dunstan's Churchyard,
Stepney, London.

★

SPUN OFF
TO THE GREAT LOOM ABOVE

Haslingden Church,
Lancashire.

★

Let this small momument record the name
Of CADMAN, and to future times proclaim
How by an attempt to fly from this high spire,
Across the Sabrine stream, he did acquire,
His fatal end. "Twas not for want of skill,
Or courage to perform the task, he fell;
No, no; a faulty cord being drawn too tight,
Hurried his soul on high to take her flight,
Which bid the body here good-night.
Feb. 2nd, 1739. Aged 28.

St. Mary's Church,
Shrewsbury.

★

V

Drinkers

Who lies here? Who do'e think?
Why, old CLAPPER WATTS, if you'll give him some drink
    Give a dead man drink? For why?
Why when he was alive he was always a-dry.

                                    Leigh Delamore Churchyard,
                                    Wiltshire.

★

Here lies JOHN STEERE,
Who, when living, brewed good beer,
Turn to the right, go down the hill,
His son keeps up the business still.

                                    St. Mary's Church,
                                    Dagenham, Essex.

★

REBECCA FREELAND
She drank good ale, good punch and wine
And lived to the age of 99.

                                    Edwallon Cemetery,
                                    Nottinghamshire.

★

This good old woman of Ryde
Ate some apples and died
The apples fermented inside the lamented
Made cider inside her inside.

Ryde Churchyard,
Isle of Wight.

★

'TWAS AS SHE TRIPT FROM CASK TO CASK
IN AT A BUNG-HOLE QUICKLY FELL,
SUFFOCATION WAS HER TASK
SHE HAD NO TIME TO SAY FAREWELL.

Kings Stanley Churchyard,
Gloucestershire.

★

Dead drunk old SUSAN oft was found;
But now she's laid beneath the ground,
As door-nail dead—alas the day!
Her nose was red, and moist as clay.
From morn to night, of care bereft,
She plied her glass, and wet her throttle,
Without a sigh her friends she left
But much she griev'd to leave her bottle.

Crowcombe Cemetery,
Somerset.

★

75

Poor JOHN SCOTT lies buried here,
Although he was both hale and stout;
Death stretched him on the bitter bier,
Now in another world he hops about.

St. George's Parish Church,
Liverpool.

★

Here lies WALTER GUNN,
Sometimes landlord of the Tun;
Sic transit gloria mundi!
He drank hard upon Friday
That being a high day,
Then took to his bed and died upon Sunday.

Blyth Cemetery,
Northumberland.

★

BENEATH THIS STONE, IN HOPES OF ZION
DOTH LIE THE LANDLORD OF THE LION:
HIS SON KEEPS ON THE BUSINESS STILL
RESIGNED UNTO THE HEAVENLY WILL.

Upton-on-Severn Cemetery,
Gloucestershire.

★

A jolly landlord once was I
And kept the Old King's Head hard by
Sold mead and gin, cider and beer,
And eke all other kinds of cheer,
Till Death my licence took away,
And put me in this house of clay:
A house at which you all must call,
Sooner or later, great or small.

> Roughtonhead Parish Church,
> Cumberland.

★

Hail! This stone marks the spot
　Where a notorious sot
　　　Doth lie;
　Whether at rest or not
　　It matters not
　　　To you or I
Oft to the "Lion" he went to fill his horn
Now to the "Grave" he's gone to get it warm.

> (Beered by public subscription by
> 　his hale and stout companions
> who deeply lament his absence).

> Tonbridge Parish Church,
> Kent.

★

JONATHAN GROBER died dead sober
Lord Thy wonders never cease.

> Clinkerton Cemetery,
> Nottinghamshire.

★

He had some faults
And many merits
He died of drinking
Ardent Spirits.

> Leamington Parish Church,
> Warwickshire.

★

The young gentleman referred to here
Killed himself by drinking October beer.
Here lie I must
Wrapp'd up in dust
Confined to be sober.
Clerk take care,
Lest you come here,
For faith here's no October.

> Middleton-in-Teesdale,
> Durham.

★

In life a jovial sot was he,
   He died from inebriate
A cup of burnt canary sack
To Earth from Heaven would bring him back.

St. George's Church,
Enfield, Middlesex.

★

JOHN ADAMS lies here, of the parish of Southwell
A carrier who carried his can to his mouth well;
He carried so much, and he carried so fast,
He could carry no more—so was carried at last!
For the liquor he drunk, being too much for one,
He could not carry-off—so he's now carri-on.

Southwell Cemetery,
Dorset.

★

My grandfather lies buried here,
   My cousin Jane, and two uncles dear;
My father perish'd with the inflammation in the thighs,
And my sister dropt down dead in the Minories.
But the reason I'm here interr'd according to my thinking
Is owing to my good living and hard drinking;
If therefore, good Christians, you wish to live long,
Don't drink too much wine, brandy, gin or anything strong.

Thetford Churchyard,
Suffolk.

79

VI

Unusual Deaths

Here lies entombed one ROGER MORTON,
Whose sudden death was early brought on!
Trying one day his corns to mow off,
The razor slipped and cut his toe off!
The toe, or rather what it grew to,
An inflammation quickly flew to;
The part then took to mortifying,
And poor dear Roger took to dying.

Acton Cemetery,
Cornwall.

★

BLOWN UPWARD
OUT OF SIGHT
HE SOUGHT THE LEAK
BY CANDLELIGHT.

Collingbourne Ducis Cemetery,
Wiltshire.

★

Here lies a man who was killed by lightening;
He died when his prospects seemed to be brightening.
He might have cut a flash in this world of trouble,
But the flash cut him and he lies in the stubble.

Great Torrington Church,
Devon.

★

Here lies JOHN BUNN
Who was killed by a gun.
His name wasn't Bunn, but his real name was Wood,
But Wood wouldn't rhyme with gun, so I thought
Bunn should.

Appleby,
Westmorland.

★

ERECTED TO THE MEMORY OF
JOHN PHILLIPS
ACCIDENTALLY SHOT AS A MARK
OF AFFECTION BY HIS BROTHER.

Finchley Cemetery,
London.

★

Beneath this stone
A lump of clay
lies Uncle PETER DANIELS
Too early in the
Month of May
He took off his
Winter flannels.

Chatham Cemetery,
Kent.

★

83

Here lyeth the body of SIMON GILKETT
Who was killed by a rockett.

> Milton Regis Parish Churchyard,
> Kent.

*

OWEN MOORE
Gone away
Owing more
Than he could pay.

> St. John's Church,
> Battersea, London.

*

Here two young Danish soldiers lie
The one in quarrell chanced to die;
The other's Head by their own law
With sword was severed at one Blow.

> St. Mary's Church, Beverley,
> Yorkshire.

*

This curious illustration of an epitaph published in 1796 shows how the punctuation of simple English sentences can make them appear to be in Latin. Ignoring the full-stops, capital letters and division of words, the sentence in fact reads: "Beneath this stone reposeth CLAUD COSTER, tripe-seller, of Impington, as doth his consort Jane."

Probably the most bizarre of all epitaphs—a memorial to a Cherry Pie! To be seen at the George Hotel, Wanstead, Essex.

In Memory of
y̨ᵉ Cherry Pey
As cost ½ a Guiney
y̨ᵉ 17 of July
That day we had good cheer
I hope to so do many a Year
RC 1752   DAᵉ Jerrey

Here two young Danish Souldiers lye
The one in quarrell chanc'd to die;
The others Head by their own Law,
With Sword was sever'd at one Blow

December the 23 d

1689

The stone marking the sad end of two Danish soldiers who quarrelled while in the service of the Prince of Orange. They rest in St. Mary's Church, Beverley, Yorkshire.

To all my friends I bid adieu
A more sudden death you never knew.
As I was leading the mare to drink
  She kicked and killed me
  Quicker'n a wink.

> Melton Mowbray Parish Church,
> Oxford.

★

Here lies an honest, independent man
  Boast more ye great ones if ye can
I have been kicked by a bull and a ram
  Now, let me lay contented as I am.

> Stalham Cemetery,
> Norfolk.

★

In memory of the Clerk's son:
  Bless my i
  Here I lies,
  In a sad pickle
  Killed by an icicle.

> Bampton Parish Church,
> Devon.

★

Here sleeps in peace a Hampshire grenadier
Who caught his death by drinking cold small beer.
Soldiers be wise from his untimely fall,
And when you're hot drink strong or none at all.

(This grave fell into disrepair and
was restored in 1781 by two officers
who added the following lines:)

An honest soldier never is forgot,
Whether he die by musket or by pot.

Cathedral Yard,
Winchester.

★

JOHN MACPHERSON was a remarkable person;
He stood 6 feet without his shoe,
And he was slew at Waterloo.

Lochmaben Church,
Dumfries.

★

Against his will
Here lies GEORGE HILL
Who from a cliff
Fell down quite stiff.

St. Joseph's Church,
Kingston-upon-Thames,
Surrey.

★

HERE LIES TWO BROTHERS
BY MISFORTUNE SURROUNDED
ONE DY'D OF HIS WOUNDS
AND THE OTHER WAS DROWNED.

> Tynemouth Cemetery,
> Northumberland.

★

Friends, cease to grieve that at Gravesend,
  My life was closed with speed,
For when the Saviour shall descend,
'Twill be graves'end indeed.

> Epitaph to a captain
> drowned at Gravesend and
> located at St. John's Churchyard
> in Horsleydown.

★

Here lies WILLIAM DEAN
Who came to this city and died
For the benefit of his health.

> Barrow Cemetery,
> Lancashire.

★

Under this stone lieth the Broken Remains of
STEPHEN JONES
Who had his leg cut off without the Consent
Of Wife or friends
On the 23rd October, 1842, in which day he died,
Aged 31 years.
Reader I bid you farewall. May the Lord have
Mercy on you in the day of trouble.

St. John's Churchyard,
Chester, Cheshire.

★

Poor MARY SNELL her's gone away;
Her would if her could
But her couldn't stay
Her had sore legs, and a baddish cough
But her legs it were that carried her off.

Chulmleigh Parish Church,
Devon.

★

Fair MAIDEN LILLYARD lies under this stone
Little was her stature, but great was her fame;
Upon the English lions she laid many thumps
And when her legs were cutted off
She fought on her stumps.

From the grave at Ancrum Moor,
Roxburgh, of a Scottish woman
who fought against the English at
Lillyard's Edge in 1545.

★

Here lies old
Aunt HANNAH PROCTER
Who purged but didn't call the Doctor.
She couldn't stay
She had to go
Praise be to God from whom
All blessings flow.

> Queenborough Cemetery,
> Medway, Kent.

★

On a Thursday she was born,
On a Thursday made a bride,
On a Thursday broke her leg,
On a Thursday put to bed, and
On a Thursday died.

> Creltow Churchyard,
> Salop, Lancashire.

★

Here lies cut down like unripe fruit
The wife of DEACON AMOS SHUTE
She died of drinking too much coffee
Anny Dominy 1840.

> Bedrule Parish Church,
> Roxburgh.

★

HERE LIES I
AND MY TWO DAUGHTERS
KILLED BY DRINKING
CHELTENHAM WATERS
IF WE HAD STUCK TO
EPSOM SALTS
WE WOULDN'T BE LYING
IN THESE VAULTS

St. Giles' Church,
Cheltenham, Gloucestershire.

★

Here lies JOHNNY COLE,
Who died, on my soul,
After eating a plentiful dinner,
While showing his crust
He was turned into dust,
With his crimes undigested, poor sinner.

Tiptree Parish Church,
Essex.

★

Here lies NED RAND, who on a sudden
Left off roast beef for hasty pudding;
Forsook old stingo, mild and stale
And every drink for Adam's ale;
Till flesh and blood reduced to batter,
Consisting of mere flour and water
Which wanting salt to keep out must

And heat to bake it to a crust,
Mouldered and crumbled into dust.

> Bedlington Church,
> Northumberland.

*

HERE LIE THE BONES,
O DONALD JONES
THE WALE O'MEN,
FOR EATING SCONES.
EATING SCONES
AND DRINKING ALE
TILL HIS LAST MOANS
HE TOOK HIS FILL.

> Skye Cemetery,
> Scotland.

*

This deceased you ne'er heard tell on
I died of eating too much mellon,
Be careful then, all you that feed, I
Suffered because I was too greedy.

> Chigwell Cemetery,
> Essex.

*

Eliza, sorrowing
Rears this marble slab
To her dear John
Who died of eating crab.

Consett Cemetery,
Durham.

★

Here lies the bones
OF JOSEPH JONES
Who ate whilst he was able;
But, once o'erfed
He dropt down dead,
And fell beneath the table.
When from the tomb,
To meet his doom,
He rises amidst sinners;
Since he must dwell
In heaven or hell,
Take him—which gives best dinners!

Wolverhampton Church,
Staffordshire.

★

Underneath this stone
Lies poor JOHN ROUND
Lost at sea
And never found.

Marple,
Derbyshire.

VII

Misers

Jemmy Wyatt

Reader, beware, of immoderate love of self;
Here lies the worst of thieves, who robbed himself.

Great Driffield Church,
Yorkshire.

★

At rest beneath this churchyard stone
    Lies stingy JEMMY WYATT;
He died one morning just at ten, and
    Saved a dinner by it.

Studley Parish Church,
Wiltshire.

★

Iron was his chest,
Iron was his door,
His head was iron,
And his heart was more.

Dunsford Cemetery,
Devon.

★

Here lyeth FATHER SPARGES,
That dyed to save the charges.

Camden Cemetery,
London.

★

Here lies JOHN MOORE, a miser old,
Who filled his cellar with silver and gold.
  Oh more, he cried, Old Moore, Old Moore,
  'Twas clear he would not close the door,
And yet he cried, oh more, Old Moore.

Yarmouth Cemetery,
Isle of Wight.

★

Stop passenger for here is laid
One who the debt of nature paid.
This is not strange, the reader cries,
  We all know here a dead man lies.
You're right; but stop, I'll tell you more:
  He never paid a debt before;
And now he's gone, I'll further say
  He never will another pay.

Corbridge Cemetery,
Northumberland.

★

GONE UNDERGROUND

> Walsall Parish Church,
> Staffordshire.

★

MARY BROOMFIELD
Dyd 19 Novr., 1755, aged 80
The chief concern of her life for the last twenty
years was to order and provide for her funeral.
Her greatest pleasure was to think and talk about it.
She lived many years on ninepence per week.

> St. Michael's Churchyard,
> Macclesfield, Cheshire.

★

To The Memory of
THOMAS HANSE
Lord, They Grace is Free Why Not For Me?
And the Lord answered and Said
Because thy debts aren't paid.

> Coggeshall Church,
> Essex.

★

Here lies one who lived unloved, and died unlamented;
Who denied plenty to himself, assistance to his friends,
        and relief to the poor;
Who starved his family, oppressed his neighbours, and
        plagued himself to gain what he
                could not enjoy;
At last, Death, more merciful to him than he was to himself
Released him from care, and his family from want;
And here he lies with the unknown he imitated, and with
                the soil he loved,
In fear of resurrection,
Lest his heirs should have spent the money he left behind,
Having laid up no treasure where moth and rust do not
        corrupt and thieves break through and
                steal.

                        Melmerby Parish Church,
                        Cumberland.

VIII

On Children

Two lovely babies lie buried here,
As ever bless'd their parents dear;
But they were seized with ague fits,
And here they lie as dead as nits.

Sunderland,
Durham.

★

THIS LITTLE HERO THAT LIES HERE,
WAS CONQUERED BY THE DIARRHEER.

St. John's Church,
Hertford.

★

JOHN CALF junior lieth here,
Without becoming Ox or Steer.

Cheriton Parish Church,
Winchester.

★

Oh cruel Death, more subtle than the Fox
To kill this CALF before he came an Ox.

Gloucester Cathedral,
Gloucestershire.

★

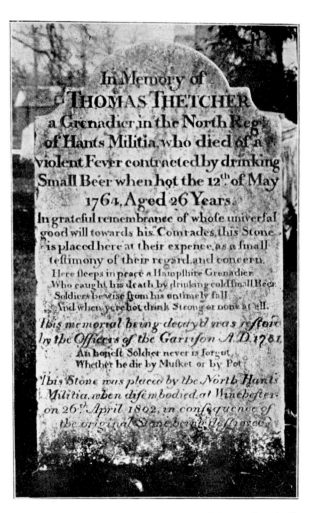

In Memory of
THOMAS THETCHER
a Grenadier in the North Reg.
of Hants Militia, who died of a
violent Fever contracted by drinking
Small Beer when hot the 12th of May
1764, Aged 26 Years.

In grateful remembrance of whose univerſal
good will towards his Comrades, this Stone
is placed here at their expence, as a ſmall
teſtimony of their regard, and concern.

Here ſleeps in peace a Hampſhire Grenadier,
Who caught his death by drinking cold ſmall Beer.
Soldiers be wiſe from his untimely fall,
And when ye're hot drink Strong or none at all.

This memorial being decay'd was reſtor'd
by the Officers of the Garriſon A.D.1781.

An honeſt Soldier never is forgot,
Whether he die by Muſket or by Pot.

This Stone was placed by the North Hants
Militia, when diſembodied at Wincheſter,
on 26th April 1802, in conſequence of
the original Stone being deſtroyed.

The soldier who died of drinking "Small Beer when hot"
—to be found in the yard at Winchester Cathedral.

The author 'researching' for material in a disused Essex grave-yard.

At the Easter end of this free
stone here doeth ly the Letle Bone of
Walter Spurrer that fine boy that was
his friends only joy. He was Drouned
at Melhams Bridg. the 20th of August
1691.

> Metalbridge Church,
> Cumberland.

★

Some have children, some have none;
Here lies the mother of 21.

> From the grave of Ann Jennings,
> in Wolstanton Cemetery,
> Cheshire.

★

Here lieth the body of NICHOLAS HOOKS of Conway, gent.,
who was the one-and-fortieth child of his father,
WILLIAM HOOKS, Esq., by ALICE his wife, and the father
of seven-and-twenty children; he died the 20th day
of March 1637.

> Aberconway Churchyard,
> Caernarvonshire.

★

Death has taken little JERRY
Son of JOSEPH and SERENA HOWELLS.
Seven days he wrestled with the dysentery
Then he perished in his little bowels.

Stow Cemetery,
Lincolnshire.

*

Here lies the body of three
Children dear
Two at Llanwonno and
One here.

Vaynor Churchyard,
nr. Merthyr Tydfil, Wales.

*

Here lies the mother of children seven,
Three on earth and four in Heaven;
The four in Heaven preferring rather
To die with mother than live with father.

Godolphin Cross Church,
Cornwall.

*

SINCE I HAVE BEEN SO
QUICKLY DONE FOR,
I WONDER WHAT I WAS
BEGUN FOR.

> Grave of an infant at
> Workington Cemetery,
> Cumberland.

★

To the memory of
JOHN MAGHI
An incomparable boy
Who, through the unskillfulness of the midwife
On the 21st day of December 1532
Was translated from the womb to the tomb.

> Highgate Cemetery,
> London.

★

Under this yew tree
Buried would I be,
For my father and me
Planted this yew tree.

> Llandidloes Cemeterv.
> Montgomeryshire.

★

IX

Grave Thoughts

Poems and epitaphs are but stuff,
Here lies BOB BARRAS and that's enough.

> Ongar Parish Church,
> Essex.

★

Here I lays
PADDY O'BLASE
With the tip of my nose
And the points of my toes
Turned up to the roots of the daisies.

> Monkstown Cemetery,
> Co. Cork.

★

I am here, I am there, do you know where?
When I was alive, 'twas that made me stare.

> Old St. Pancras Cemetery,
> Middlesex.

★

Here lieth Sir Thomas Jay, Knight,
Who, being dead, I upon his grave did shite.

> Lines subsequently engraved on
> the tomb of a J.P. at Poole,
> Dorset, by an aggrieved criminal.

★

Here lies JOHN ROSS
Kicked by a Hoss.

> Kendal Parish Church,
> Westmorland.

★

In this grave you see before you,
  Lies buried up a dismal story
A YOUNG MAIDEN
She was crossed in love and
  Taken to the realms above.
But he that crossed her
  I should say
Deserves to go the other way.

> Pentewan Graveyard,
> Cornwall.

★

HERE I LIE, AT THE CHANCEL DOOR,
HERE I LIE, BECAUSE I'M POOR
THE FARTHER IN, THE MORE YOU PAY
HERE I LIE AS WARM AS THEY,

> Kingsbridge Parish Church,
> Devon.

★

THORPE'S
CORPSE

> Sherburn Cemetery,
> Durham.

★

Underneath this humble stone,
Sleeps a skull, of name unknown.
Deep in Eden's Bed twas found,
Was ye luckless owner drowned?
What matter since we all must die,
Whether death be wet or dry!

> Kendal Graveyard,
> Westmorland.

★

At my right hand lies my son JOHN
   As we did lay in bed;
And there do lay till Christ do say,
   "Come out ye dead".

Bishop Cumming's Churchyard,
Wiltshire.

★

True to his King, his country was his glory,
   When Bony won, he said it was a story.

The gravestone of patriot
Samuel Cleater at Kirk Hallam
Cemetery, Derbyshire.

★

Edward	EDWARD LAMBE	Lambe
Ever	second sonne of	Lived
Envied	*Thomas Lambe,*	Laudably
Evill	*of Trimley,*	Lord
Endured	Esquire	Lett
Extremities	All his days	Like
Even	he lived a Bachelor	Life
Earnestly	Well learned in Deveyne	Learne
Expecting	and Common Lawes,	Ledede
Eternal	with his councell he	Livers
Ease	helped many, yett took	Lament.
	fees scarse of any.	

He dyed the 19th November, 1647.

East Berghott Church,
Suffolk.

★

113

TWO LITTLEBOYS LIE HERE
YET STRANGE TO SAY
THESE LITTLEBOYS
ARE GIRLS

> From the tomb of Emma and
> Maria Littleboy at Hornsey
> Cemetery, London.

★

Here lyes the bodeys of GEORGE YOUNG and all their
posterity for more than fifty years backwards.

> Montrose Cemetery,
> Scotland.

★

Here lies the body of WILLIAM STRATTON, of
Paddington, buried 18th day of May, 1743 aged
97 years; who had by his first wife 28 children;
by his second 17; was own father to 45; grandfather to 86; great-grandfather to 23. In all
154 children.

> Hyden Churchyard,
> Yorkshire.

★

Doth worm eat Worme? Knight Worme this truth confirms,
For here, with worms, lies Worme, a dish for worms.
Doth worm eat Worme? Sure Worme will this deny,
For Worme with worms, a dish for worms don't lie.
'Tis so, and 'tis not so, for free from worms
'Tis certain Worme is blest without his worms.

> Tomb of St. Richard Worme in
> Peterborough Cathedral.

★

Underneath this pile of stones,
Lies all that's left of Sally Jones,
Her name was BRIGGS, it was not JONES,
But JONES was used to rhyme with stones.

> Blackburn,
> Lancashire.

★

Grim death
To please his palate
Has taken my lettuce
To put in his sallat.

> Epitaph to Letitia, an Ipswich,
> Suffolk, farmer's daughter.

★

Though LONG, yet short,
Though short, yet *pretty* Long.

> From the grave of a Miss Long,
> who was very beautiful, but so
> small she was called the
> "Pocket Venus", in Finchley
> Cemetery, London.

★

Stranger pause and shed a tear
For MARY JANE lies buried here
Mingled in a most surprising manner
With SUSAN, JOY and portions of HANNAH.

> From a stone placed over the
> spot where urns containing the
> ashes of four wives were over-
> turned in a storm. Ringwood
> Parish Church, Kent.

★

Here lies the body of THOMAS PARR;
What, old Tom? No!
What, young Tom? Ah!

> Swaffham Churchyard,
> Norfolk.

★

NOTT BORN
NOTT DEAD
NOTT CHRISTENED
NOTT BEGOT
LOW HERE SHE LIES
WHO WAS
AND WHO WAS NOTT.

> Grave of a Mrs. Nott at Hadding-
> ton Cemetery, Lincolnshire.

★

Here, in this Grace, there lies a CAVE:
  We call a Cave a Grave.
If Cave be Grave, and Grave be Cave,
  Then reader, judge, I crave,
Whether doth Cave lye here in Grave
  Or Grave here lie in Cave:
If Grave in Cave here buried lye,
Then, Grave, where is thy victory?
  Go, reader! and report
  Here lies a Cave who conquers Death,
  And buries his own Grave.

> The grave of Theophilus Cave
> in Barrow-upon-Soar Church,
> Leicestershire.

★

In a vault underneath this stone
Lie several of the SAUNDERS,
Late of this Parish.
Particulars the Last Day will disclose.

> Tetbury Church,
> Gloucestershire.

★

117

If your nose is close to the grindstone
  And you hold it there long enough
In time you'll say there's no such thing
As brooks that babble and birds that sing
These three will all your world compose—
Just you, the stone and your poor old nose.

Falsgrave Parish Church,
nr. Scarborough, Yorkshire.

★

HERE LIES THE REMAINS OF

S. W. EILLITON,

WHO DURING THE BOER WAR, SUFFERED
AN INJURY CAUSING COMPLETE
AND UTTER IMMOBILITY. BUT SOME-
HOW RAN AND CAUGHT UP, AND KEPT
AHEAD OF, THE MANY STRESSES AND
STAINS OF THIS HECTIC LIFE.

Avebury Cemetery,
Wiltshire.

★

This empty urn is sacred to the memory of
JOHN WENDING
Who died abroad in Finistere
If he had lived
He would have been buried here.

Conemara,
Ireland.

★

JOHN PALFRYMAN, which lieth here,
    Was aged twenty-four year;
And near this place his brother lies,
    Also his father when he dies.

> Grantham Parish Church,
> Lincolnshire.

★

Here lies JOHN HIGLEY whose father and mother
Were drowned in their passage from America.
Had they both lived they would have been buried here.

> Belturbet Churchyard,
> Ireland.

★

Life is an inn upon a market day:
Some short-pursed pilgrims breakfast and away;
Some do to dinner stay, and get full fed,
And others after supper steal to bed;
Large are the bills who linger out the day,
The shortest stayers had the least to pay.

> Dalston Churchyard,
> nr. Carlisle, Cumberland.

★

The Charnel mounted on this w
Sets to be seen in funer
A matron playn domestic
In housewifery a princip
In care and payns continu
Not slow, nor gay, nor prodig   } ALL
Yet neighbourly and hospitib
Her children seven yet living
Her sixty-seventh year hence did c
To rest her body natur
In hope to rise spiritu

Epitaph on an Alderman's wife,
Ellen Reson, in Hadleigh Church,
Suffolk.

★

Where I am gone, you are coming;
So be serious, stop your funning.

> Winstone Churchyard,
> Yorkshire.

★

Here I lie and no wonder I'm dead,
For the wheel of the waggon went over my head.

> Prendergast Churchyard,
> Pembrokeshire.

★

Reader, if cash thou art in want of any,
Dig five feet deep and you will find a PENNY.

> From the grave of a Mrs Penney
> in Witnesham Parish Church,
> Suffolk.

★

How strange, yet true, that full seventy years
Was his wife happy in her tears!

> Tomb of Daniel Tear at Santon
> Cumberland.

★

X

Short—But Not Always Sweet

Here lies JOHN and his wife
JANET McFEE
40 hee — 30 shee.

St. John's Churchyard,
Edinburgh.

*

But here to earth again it goes,
From earth my body first arose
I never desire to have it more
To plague me as it did before.

Llangerrig Churchyard,
Montgomeryshire.

*

Within this tomb lies the world's loveliest rose
But she who was sweet will now offend your nose.

Godstow Church,
nr. Oxford.

*

Visitors tread gently
Here lies DOCTOR BENTLEY.

Great Haywood Churchyard,
Staffordshire.

*

To the memory of JOSEPH LEE, who died in 1825, aged
103 years.

Joseph Lee is dead and gone,
We ne'er shall see him more;
He used to wear an old drab coat
All buttoned down before.

Mathern Churchyard, Chepstow,
London.

*

Here lyeth ye body of
SARAH BLOOMFIELD,
Aged 74
Cut off in Blooming yuthe, we can but pity.

St. John's Church, Yarmouth,
Isle of Wight.

*

Here lies SIR JOHN PLUMPUDDING of the Grange,
Who hanged himself one morning for a change.

North Country
(Probably Northumberland.)

*

HERE LIES JANE SHORE
I SAY NO MORE
WHO WAS ALIVE
IN SIXTY-FIVE.

Wrexham Parish Church,
Cheshire.

*

In Memory of Sarah WiLLock WiFe of
John Willock. Wo Died August 15,
1825, Aged 48 years, She was But
Reason ForBids me to Sa what But
think what a woman should Be and
she was that.

Monkseaton Churchyard,
Northumberland.

*

Here lies the body of MARY GWYNNE,
Who was so very pure within,
She cracked the shell of earthly skin
And hatched herself a cherubim.

Chesterton Cemetery,
nr. Cambridge.

*

Death will'd that WILLING here should lie,
Although *unwilling* he to die.

> Tombstone of William Willing
> at Bradford, Yorkshire.

★

Here lies JOHN ADAMS, who received a thump
Right on the forehead, from the parish pump,
Which gave him the quietus in the end,
For many doctors did his case attend.

> Ulverston Graveyard,
> Cumberland.

★

Grim Death took me without any warning,
I was well at night, and died at nine in the morning.

> Sevenoaks Churchyard,
> Kent.

★

Born in America, In Europe bred,
In Africa travell'd, and in Asia dead.

> Wrexham Church,
> Denbighshire.

★

Here lies the wife of SIMON STOKES
Who lived and died — like other folks.

> Bowness,
> Westmorland.

★

Here lies the body of JOHN TROLLOPE
Whose hands made these stones to roll up;
When God Almighty took his soul up
His body went to fill the hole up.

> Thornton Churchyard,
> Yorkshire.

★

He lived one hundred and five,
Sanguine and strong;
A hundred to five
You live not so long.

> Brightwell Churchyard,
> Oxfordshire.

★

Here lies JANE KITCHEN
Who when her glass was spent
She kickt up her heels,
And away she went.

> Bury St. Edmunds Parish
> Church, Suffolk.

★

In this churchyard lies EPPIE COUTTS
Either here or hereabouts:
But whaur it is none can tell
Till Eppie rise and tell hersel'.

> Torryburn Churchyard,
> nr. Dunfermline, Scotland.

★

Here lies PAT STEEL
That's very true.
Who was he? What was he?
What's that to you?

> Mortlake Cemetery,
> London.

★

Oh, stranger, pause and give one sigh,
For the sake of him who here doth lie,
Beneath this little mound of earth
Two thousand miles from land of birth.

> Grave of John Robertson, an
> American, at Dalry, Kirkcudbright,
> Scotland.

★

Sudden and unexpected was the end
Of our esteemed and beloved friend:
He gave to all his friends a sudden shock,
By one day falling into Sunderland Dock.

Whitby Churchyard,
Yorkshire.

★

Remember me as you pass by
As you are now, so once was I,
As I am now, you soon will be,
Therefore prepare to follow me.

(To this was later added:)

To follow you I'm not content
Until I know which way you went.

Great Burstead Church,
Essex.

★

The wedding day appointed was
And wedding clothes provided,
But ere that day did come, alas!
He sickened and he dieded.

Bideford Churchyard,
Devon.

★

Here lies one, a sailor's bride,
Who widowed was because of the tide;
It drowned her husband—so she died.

St. Nicholas Churchyard,
Yarmouth.

★

This tombstone is a Milestone;
   Hah! how so?
Because beneath lies Miles, who's
   Miles below.

Windermere Cemetery,
Westmorland.

★

Nineteen years a maid,
Two years a wife
Nine days a mother
And then departed life.

Bidston Parish Church,
Birkenhead, Lancashire.

★

Beneath this stone I do entrust,
Are the remnants of her worthy dust:
Farewell awhile, ye silent tomb,
Until your husband calls for room.

Hanwell Churchyard,
Middlesex.

★

Pain was my portion,
Physic was my food;
Groans my devotion;
Drugs did me no good.

Oldbury-on-Severn Church,
Gloucestershire.

★

Here lies the body of THOMAS PROCTER,
Who lived and died without a doctor.

Luton Church,
Bedfordshire.

★

Curious enough, we all must say,
That what was STONE should now be clay:
More curious still, to own we must,
That what was STONE will soon be dust.

Epitaph on a Mr. Stone,
Walworth Church, London.

★

Here lieth the body of ELIZABETH ADDISON
—JOHN, her son,
And old ROGER to come.

Whittlesea Churchyard,
Ely.

★

HERE LIES A FATHER OF 29
THERE WOULD HAVE BEEN MORE
BUT HE DIDN'T HAVE TIME.

Southport,
Lancashire.

★

We must all die, there is no doubt;
Your glass is running—mine is out.

Shoreditch Churchyard,
London.

★

132

Life's but a jest,
And all things show it;
I thought so once,
But now I know it.

Newington Churchyard,
Kent.

★

Death will'd that Willing here should lie,
Although unwilling he to die.

Epitaph on William Willing at
Melton Mowbray, Suffolk.

★

SHALL	WEE	ALL	DIE.
WEE	SHALL	DIE	ALL.
ALL	DIE?	SHALL	WEE?
DIE	ALL	WEE	SHALL.

Cunwallow, nr. Helstone,
Cornwall.

★

As you are in health and spirits gay,
I was, too, the other day;
I thought myself of life as safe
As those that read my epitaph.

Byfield Church,
Northamptonshire.

★

133

Praises on tombs are trifles vainly spent,
A man's good name is his best monument.

> Caermarthen Churchyard,
> Wales.

★

Live well—die never:
Die well—live for ever.

> Kingston Churchyard,
> Hampshire.

★

FINIS

*—which is also the epitaph on
a London actor buried in
Highgate Cemetery, London.*

ACKNOWLEDGEMENTS

I should like to offer my thanks to the many generous friends who contributed ideas, suggestions and actual material to this collection. To name them all, and indeed all the newspapers, magazines and books from which the epitaphs came, would take up more space than is justified and I hope that it will suffice for me to simply acknowledge with graditude all they have donated.

By name, though, I must record my thanks to Spike Milligan for his Introduction so readily given, Frank Graham for his enthusiasm for the project, and my wife, Philippa, for a lot of encouragement and painstaking typing. It has all been great fun—and I trust the result will give you, the reader, some pleasure, too.

Gravely Yours,
Peter Haining.